Copyright © 2023 by S. J. Matthews (Author)

This book is protected by copyright law and is intended solely for personal use. Reproduction, distribution, or any other form of use requires the written permission of the author. The information presented in this book is for educational and entertainment purposes only, and while every effort has been made to ensure its accuracy and completeness, no guarantees are made. The author is not providing legal, financial, medical, or professional advice, and readers should consult with a licensed professional before implementing any of the techniques discussed in this book. The content in this book has been sourced from various reliable sources, but readers should exercise their own judgment when using this information. The author is not responsible for any losses, direct or indirect, that may occur from the use of this book, including but not limited to errors, omissions, or inaccuracies.

We hope this book has been informative and helpful on your journey to understanding and celebrating older adults. Thank you for your interest and support!

Title: Decentralized Governance and 51% Attack Mitigation in Blockchain Networks

Subtitle: Mastering Prevention

Series: Defending Bitcoin: A Comprehensive Guide to 51% Attack Prevention

By S. J. Matthews

"Bitcoin is a remarkable cryptographic achievement and the ability to create something that is not duplicable in the digital world has enormous value."
Eric Schmidt, Former CEO of Google

"Bitcoin is a technological tour de force."
Bill Gates, Co-Founder of Microsoft

"Bitcoin is the beginning of something great: a currency without a government, something necessary and imperative."
Nassim Taleb, Author of "The Black Swan"

"Bitcoin is a remarkable cryptographic achievement... The ability to create something which is not duplicable in the digital world has enormous value."
Roger Ver, Bitcoin Investor and Entrepreneur

"Bitcoin is a remarkable cryptographic achievement and the ability to create something that is not duplicable in the digital world has enormous value."
Peter Thiel, Co-Founder of PayPal

"Bitcoin is a very exciting development, it might lead to a world currency. I think over the next decade it will grow to become one of the most important ways to pay for things and transfer assets."
Kim Dotcom, Founder of Megaupload

"Bitcoin is a protocol that could change the world, like the web did. Don't miss out."
Andreas Antonopoulos, Bitcoin Educator and Author

"Bitcoin is better than currency in that you don't have to be physically in the same place and, of course, for large transactions, currency can get pretty inconvenient."
Bill Gates, Co-Founder of Microsoft

Table of Contents

Introduction 7
The importance of Bitcoin mining in maintaining the integrity of the blockchain 7
Overview of the book's contents 9
How mining rewards incentivize miners to secure the network 12

Chapter 1: The Basics of Bitcoin Mining 15
How Bitcoin mining works 15
The role of miners in the network 18
The block reward and mining difficulty 21
Mining hardware and software 24

Chapter 2: Mining Pools and Cloud Mining 27
Advantages and disadvantages of mining pools 27
How mining pools work 30
Cloud mining and its risks 34

Chapter 3: Mining Economics and Profitability 37
The costs of mining Bitcoin 37
Calculating mining profitability 41
Factors that impact mining profitability 44
Long-term mining incentives and the halving 48

Chapter 4: The Environmental Impact of Bitcoin Mining 51
Energy consumption and carbon emissions 51

    Renewable energy and its role in Bitcoin mining 54

    Criticisms and misconceptions about Bitcoin mining's environmental impact 58

Chapter 5: Alternative Consensus Mechanisms 61

    Overview of proof-of-stake and other consensus algorithms 61

    Advantages and disadvantages of alternative consensus mechanisms 65

    Potential future developments in blockchain consensus. 68

Conclusion 71

    Review of the book's key takeaways 71

    Final thoughts on the importance of Bitcoin mining 73

    Encouragement to learn more and get involved in the Bitcoin community 77

Key Terms and Definitions 79

Supporting Materials 82

Introduction

The importance of Bitcoin mining in maintaining the integrity of the blockchain

Bitcoin mining plays a crucial role in maintaining the integrity of the blockchain network. It is the process by which new transactions are verified and added to the blockchain, ensuring that the network is secure, decentralized, and resistant to tampering. Without mining, the Bitcoin network would not be able to function as a decentralized digital currency, and it would be vulnerable to fraudulent activities.

The importance of Bitcoin mining in maintaining the integrity of the blockchain can be seen in several key ways:

1. Verifying Transactions: Bitcoin miners verify new transactions on the network by solving complex mathematical problems, which require significant computational power. This process ensures that every new transaction is legitimate and that no double-spending or other fraudulent activities occur. Without this verification process, the integrity of the blockchain would be compromised, and the network would not be trustworthy.

2. Creating New Bitcoins: Bitcoin miners are also responsible for creating new Bitcoins by solving the mathematical problems required to add new blocks to the

blockchain. This reward incentivizes miners to continue mining and securing the network, ensuring that the network remains decentralized and secure.

3. Maintaining Network Security: The computational power required for Bitcoin mining makes it very difficult for any individual or group to gain control over the network. This means that the Bitcoin network is highly resistant to attacks and tampering, ensuring that transactions remain secure and private.

4. Ensuring Decentralization: Bitcoin mining is a decentralized process, which means that no single entity can control or manipulate the network. This decentralization is critical to the integrity of the blockchain, as it ensures that no individual or group can compromise the network's security.

In conclusion, Bitcoin mining plays a crucial role in maintaining the integrity of the blockchain network. It ensures that transactions are verified, new Bitcoins are created, and the network remains secure, decentralized, and resistant to tampering. Without mining, the Bitcoin network would not be able to function as a decentralized digital currency, and it would be vulnerable to fraudulent activities.

Overview of the book's contents

This book takes a psychological approach to understanding the motivations and behavior of hackers and attackers who carry out 51% attacks on the Bitcoin network. It explores factors such as risk tolerance, moral reasoning, and group dynamics. In addition, this book also discusses the importance of Bitcoin mining in maintaining the integrity of the blockchain and explores the different aspects of Bitcoin mining, including its economics, environmental impact, and alternative consensus mechanisms.

Overview of the book's contents:

Chapter 1: The Basics of Bitcoin Mining This chapter provides an overview of how Bitcoin mining works, the role of miners in the network, and the block reward and mining difficulty. It also covers the different types of mining hardware and software that are used for Bitcoin mining.

Chapter 2: Mining Pools and Cloud Mining This chapter explores the advantages and disadvantages of mining pools, which are groups of miners who work together to solve blocks and share the rewards. It also discusses cloud mining, which is a form of mining that allows individuals to rent mining equipment from remote data centers.

Chapter 3: Mining Economics and Profitability This chapter covers the costs of mining Bitcoin, how to calculate mining profitability, and the factors that impact mining profitability. It also discusses the long-term mining incentives and the halving, which is the process by which the block reward is reduced by half every 210,000 blocks.

Chapter 4: The Environmental Impact of Bitcoin Mining This chapter explores the energy consumption and carbon emissions associated with Bitcoin mining. It also covers renewable energy and its role in Bitcoin mining, as well as criticisms and misconceptions about Bitcoin mining's environmental impact.

Chapter 5: Alternative Consensus Mechanisms This chapter provides an overview of alternative consensus mechanisms, such as proof-of-stake, and discusses the advantages and disadvantages of each mechanism. It also explores potential future developments in blockchain consensus.

Chapter 6: Understanding the Mindset of Hackers and Attackers This chapter takes a psychological approach to understanding the motivations and behavior of hackers and attackers who carry out 51% attacks on the Bitcoin network. It explores factors such as risk tolerance, moral reasoning, and group dynamics.

Chapter 7: 51% Attack Mitigation in Blockchain Networks This chapter covers the different strategies that can be used to mitigate the risk of 51% attacks on blockchain networks. It also explores the role of decentralized governance in ensuring the security of the network.

Conclusion: In conclusion, this book provides a comprehensive overview of Bitcoin mining, its economics, environmental impact, and alternative consensus mechanisms. It also takes a psychological approach to understanding the motivations and behavior of hackers and attackers who carry out 51% attacks on the Bitcoin network, and explores strategies for mitigating the risk of these attacks. The book emphasizes the importance of Bitcoin mining in maintaining the integrity of the blockchain and encourages readers to learn more and get involved in the Bitcoin community.

How mining rewards incentivize miners to secure the network

Bitcoin is a decentralized digital currency that operates on a peer-to-peer network. It relies on a group of miners to secure the network and validate transactions. In exchange for their efforts, miners receive a block reward, which is currently 6.25 BTC per block. This reward incentivizes miners to continue mining and ensures the security and integrity of the blockchain. In this chapter, we will explore how mining rewards incentivize miners to secure the network.

The Role of Miners in the Network:

Miners are responsible for adding new transactions to the blockchain and creating new blocks. Each block contains a group of transactions, and the miner who creates the block receives a reward in the form of new bitcoins. The block reward is the main incentive for miners to continue mining and maintain the security of the network.

The Block Reward and Mining Difficulty:

The block reward is currently 6.25 BTC per block. However, the block reward is reduced by half every 210,000 blocks, or approximately every four years. This process is known as the halving, and it ensures that the total number of bitcoins in circulation will never exceed 21 million. As the block reward decreases, miners are incentivized to continue mining by the transaction fees that are included in each block.

Mining Hardware and Software:

Mining hardware and software are essential components of the mining process. Miners use specialized hardware, such as ASICs, to solve complex mathematical problems and create new blocks. Mining software allows miners to connect to the Bitcoin network and manage their mining operations.

Calculating Mining Profitability:

Mining profitability is calculated by subtracting the costs of mining from the revenue generated by mining. The costs of mining include electricity, hardware, and maintenance costs. The revenue generated by mining includes the block reward and transaction fees. Miners must ensure that their mining operations are profitable in order to continue mining and maintain the security of the network.

Long-Term Mining Incentives and the Halving:

As the block reward decreases over time, miners are incentivized to continue mining by the transaction fees that are included in each block. Transaction fees are paid by users who want their transactions to be processed quickly. Miners prioritize transactions with higher fees, which ensures that the network is efficient and reliable.

Conclusion:

In conclusion, mining rewards incentivize miners to secure the network and maintain the integrity of the blockchain. The block reward is the main incentive for miners to continue mining, and the halving ensures that the total number of bitcoins in circulation will never exceed 21 million. As the block reward decreases, miners are incentivized to continue mining by transaction fees. Mining hardware and software are essential components of the mining process, and miners must ensure that their operations are profitable in order to continue mining.

Chapter 1: The Basics of Bitcoin Mining
How Bitcoin mining works

Bitcoin mining is the process of adding new transactions to the blockchain and creating new blocks. In this chapter, we will explore how Bitcoin mining works.

How Bitcoin Mining Works:

Bitcoin mining is a complex process that involves solving complex mathematical problems in order to create new blocks. When a new transaction is broadcast to the network, it is added to a pool of unconfirmed transactions. Miners compete to solve a cryptographic puzzle associated with the transaction data, and the first miner to solve the puzzle receives a block reward in the form of new bitcoins.

The cryptographic puzzle that miners must solve is called a proof of work. A proof of work is a piece of data that is difficult to produce but easy to verify. In the case of Bitcoin, miners must produce a hash that meets a certain set of criteria. The hash must be less than or equal to a specific target value that is determined by the mining difficulty. The mining difficulty is adjusted every 2016 blocks, or approximately every two weeks, in order to maintain a target block time of 10 minutes.

In order to solve the proof of work, miners use specialized hardware, such as ASICs, that are designed to perform the specific calculations required by the mining algorithm. The hardware is connected to the Bitcoin network, and the mining software communicates with other nodes on the network in order to receive new transactions and broadcast new blocks.

When a miner successfully solves a proof of work, they create a new block that contains a group of transactions. The block is broadcast to the network, and other nodes on the network verify the validity of the block. If the block is valid, it is added to the blockchain, and the miner who created the block receives a block reward in the form of new bitcoins.

The Role of Miners in the Network:

Miners play an essential role in the Bitcoin network. They are responsible for adding new transactions to the blockchain and creating new blocks. Without miners, the network would be unable to process transactions and maintain the integrity of the blockchain.

Mining Rewards and Incentives:

As mentioned earlier, miners receive a block reward in the form of new bitcoins for each block that they create. The current block reward is 6.25 BTC per block, and it is reduced by half every 210,000 blocks, or approximately every four years. The block reward is the main incentive for miners to continue mining, and it ensures the security and integrity of the blockchain.

In addition to the block reward, miners also receive transaction fees for including transactions in their blocks. Transaction fees are paid by users who want their transactions to be processed quickly. Miners prioritize transactions with higher fees, which ensures that the network is efficient and reliable.

Conclusion:

In conclusion, Bitcoin mining is the process of adding new transactions to the blockchain and creating new blocks. Miners use specialized hardware and software to solve complex mathematical problems and create new blocks. The block reward and transaction fees are the main incentives for miners to continue mining, and they ensure the security and integrity of the blockchain.

The role of miners in the network

Miners are an integral part of the Bitcoin network, serving as the backbone of the blockchain. Without miners, Bitcoin transactions would not be validated and confirmed, rendering the network useless. In this section, we will discuss the important role miners play in the Bitcoin network.

Verification of Transactions

Miners validate Bitcoin transactions by solving complex mathematical algorithms, which adds the transaction to the blockchain. This process requires powerful computing equipment and electricity, which is why miners are compensated for their efforts. Miners also play a role in ensuring the accuracy and integrity of the blockchain by verifying transactions and rejecting any fraudulent ones.

Adding New Blocks

In addition to validating transactions, miners add new blocks to the blockchain. Each block contains a list of recently validated transactions, and miners must solve a complex mathematical puzzle to add the block to the chain. This process is known as mining a block, and it requires a significant amount of computational power. Miners are rewarded with Bitcoin for successfully mining a new block, which is an important incentive for miners to continue supporting the network.

Maintaining Network Security

Miners are also responsible for maintaining the security of the Bitcoin network. As more miners join the network, the computational power required to mine new blocks increases, making it more difficult for malicious actors to launch an attack. The decentralized nature of the Bitcoin network also makes it difficult for any single entity to control the network, as it would require a majority of the mining power.

Ensuring Consensus

Consensus is crucial in the Bitcoin network, as it ensures that all transactions are validated and recorded accurately. Miners play a critical role in achieving consensus by verifying transactions and adding new blocks to the blockchain. As long as the majority of miners agree on the validity of a transaction or block, it is considered valid and added to the blockchain. This ensures that the network remains secure and free from fraudulent activity.

Conclusion

In conclusion, miners are essential to the functioning of the Bitcoin network. They validate transactions, add new blocks to the blockchain, maintain network security, and ensure consensus. Without miners, the network would be vulnerable to attack, fraudulent activity, and would ultimately lose its value. It is therefore crucial to understand the role of miners in the network and the incentives that drive them to support it.

The block reward and mining difficulty

The block reward and mining difficulty are two important concepts in Bitcoin mining that affect the incentives and profitability of miners. In this section, we will discuss these concepts in detail and their impact on the Bitcoin network.

Block Reward

The block reward is the amount of Bitcoin that is given to the miner who successfully mines a new block and adds it to the blockchain. This reward serves as an incentive for miners to continue supporting the network, as it allows them to earn a profit from their mining efforts. When the Bitcoin network first launched, the block reward was 50 BTC per block. However, this reward is halved every 210,000 blocks, which occurs approximately every four years.

The current block reward is 6.25 BTC per block, and it is expected to continue halving until it reaches zero, which is estimated to occur around the year 2140. This reduction in block rewards means that miners must rely increasingly on transaction fees to earn a profit from their mining efforts. As the number of transactions on the Bitcoin network increases, so too does the potential for miners to earn higher transaction fees.

Mining Difficulty

Mining difficulty is a measure of how difficult it is to mine a new block on the Bitcoin network. The Bitcoin network adjusts the mining difficulty every 2,016 blocks, or roughly every two weeks, to ensure that new blocks are added to the blockchain at a consistent rate of approximately one block every 10 minutes. If mining difficulty is too high, it can make it difficult for miners to mine new blocks and earn a profit. Conversely, if mining difficulty is too low, it can lead to an oversupply of new blocks and devalue Bitcoin.

Mining difficulty is adjusted based on the total computational power of the network, which is referred to as the hash rate. If the hash rate increases, the mining difficulty will also increase to maintain the consistent rate of block creation. Conversely, if the hash rate decreases, the mining difficulty will decrease to maintain the block creation rate.

Impact on Miners

The block reward and mining difficulty have a significant impact on the profitability of Bitcoin mining. As the block reward decreases, miners must rely more heavily on transaction fees to earn a profit. This means that miners must be strategic in choosing which transactions to include in a block, as higher transaction fees will yield higher profits.

Mining difficulty also affects profitability, as it can make it more difficult for miners to mine new blocks and earn rewards. However, it can also create opportunities for miners who have invested in more powerful and efficient mining equipment, as they will have a greater chance of successfully mining new blocks.

Conclusion

The block reward and mining difficulty are important concepts in Bitcoin mining that affect the incentives and profitability of miners. The decreasing block reward means that miners must rely more heavily on transaction fees to earn a profit, while mining difficulty ensures a consistent rate of block creation. As the Bitcoin network continues to evolve, these concepts will continue to shape the mining landscape and the overall health of the network.

Mining hardware and software

Mining hardware and software are essential components in the Bitcoin mining process. In this section, we will discuss the various types of mining hardware and software available, their features, and their importance in mining.

Mining Hardware: Mining hardware is specialized equipment used to mine Bitcoins. In the early days of Bitcoin mining, miners used a standard CPU to mine Bitcoins. However, as the difficulty of mining increased, specialized hardware was developed to mine Bitcoins more efficiently. The following are the most common types of mining hardware:

1. CPU (Central Processing Unit) Mining: A CPU is a general-purpose processor that is the most basic type of mining hardware. However, it is not efficient for mining Bitcoin due to its low hash rate.

2. GPU (Graphics Processing Unit) Mining: GPUs are more efficient than CPUs for mining. They are faster and can handle more calculations per second. This makes them more suitable for mining Bitcoin.

3. ASIC (Application-Specific Integrated Circuit) Mining: ASICs are specialized hardware designed specifically for mining Bitcoin. They are highly efficient and offer the

highest hash rates. However, they are also the most expensive.

Mining Software: Mining software is a program that connects the mining hardware to the Bitcoin network. The software allows miners to receive work from the Bitcoin network and submit their solutions. The following are the most common types of mining software:

1. CGMiner: CGMiner is one of the most popular mining software used for Bitcoin mining. It is open-source and supports multiple platforms such as Windows, Linux, and Mac.

2. BFGMiner: BFGMiner is another popular mining software that supports ASIC and FPGA mining hardware. It is also open-source and supports multiple platforms.

3. EasyMiner: EasyMiner is a GUI-based mining software that is easy to use. It supports both CPU and GPU mining and is available for Windows, Linux, and Android.

4. BitMinter: BitMinter is a mining pool that provides its own mining software. The software supports ASIC and FPGA mining hardware and is available for Windows, Linux, and Mac.

Conclusion: Mining hardware and software are crucial components in the Bitcoin mining process. Choosing the right mining hardware and software is essential for mining

Bitcoin efficiently and profitably. As the difficulty of mining increases, it is essential to keep up with the latest hardware and software developments to remain competitive in the mining market.

Chapter 2: Mining Pools and Cloud Mining

Advantages and disadvantages of mining pools

Mining pools are a popular method of Bitcoin mining in which multiple miners combine their computing power to increase their chances of solving a block and receiving a reward. While mining pools offer several advantages, they also have some disadvantages.

Advantages:

1. Increased chances of earning rewards: One of the most significant advantages of mining pools is that they increase the chances of earning rewards. Since multiple miners combine their resources, they can solve blocks faster and more frequently, leading to a more predictable and steady stream of rewards.

2. Reduced variance: Bitcoin mining can be a highly volatile and unpredictable activity. Even with high-end hardware, individual miners can go days or even weeks without earning a reward. Mining pools help reduce this variance, ensuring more consistent earnings for participants.

3. Lower barrier to entry: For small-scale miners, joining a mining pool can be a more accessible way to participate in Bitcoin mining. Instead of having to invest in expensive hardware and compete with larger mining

operations, they can simply join a pool and contribute their computing power.

4. More predictable income: Mining pools generally distribute rewards to members based on their contributions to the pool's computing power. This means that participants can have a more predictable income stream, rather than the potentially lumpy earnings of solo mining.

Disadvantages:

1. Higher fees: Mining pools typically charge fees for their services, which can eat into the rewards earned by participants. These fees can vary widely and can be structured in various ways, such as a percentage of earnings or a flat fee per block.

2. Centralization: Mining pools can contribute to the centralization of Bitcoin mining, as larger pools can control a significant portion of the network's computing power. This concentration of power can lead to concerns about the security and decentralization of the network.

3. Reduced control: When participating in a mining pool, individual miners have less control over which transactions they include in blocks. This can be a concern for those who prioritize the inclusion of certain types of transactions, such as those with higher fees.

4. Dependence on pool operator: Mining pools are typically run by a central operator, and participants must trust that operator to distribute rewards fairly and to act in the best interests of the pool's members. There have been cases of pool operators behaving dishonestly or engaging in fraudulent activities, leading to the loss of earnings for participants.

In conclusion, mining pools offer several advantages for Bitcoin miners, including increased chances of earning rewards and reduced variance in earnings. However, they also have some significant drawbacks, such as higher fees and concerns about centralization and reduced control over which transactions are included in blocks. It is essential for miners to carefully consider these factors when deciding whether to join a mining pool or mine solo.

How mining pools work

Mining pools have become an essential part of the Bitcoin mining process, especially for individual miners. A mining pool is a group of miners who combine their computational resources to increase their chances of solving a block and receiving the block reward. In this section, we will discuss how mining pools work and their various components.

Mining Pool Basics To understand how mining pools work, it is important to first understand how the Bitcoin mining process works. As we discussed earlier, Bitcoin mining involves solving complex mathematical problems that validate transactions and add them to the blockchain. Miners use powerful computers and specialized hardware to perform these calculations and compete with each other to solve the problem and earn a reward.

In a mining pool, multiple miners combine their computing power to increase their chances of solving the problem and earning the block reward. Instead of competing against each other, they work together to find a solution. Once a block is solved, the reward is split among the pool members, based on their contribution to the pool's total computational power.

Mining Pool Components Mining pools are composed of several different components, each with its own function. The main components of a mining pool are:

1. Pool Server: The pool server is responsible for managing the pool and distributing work to the individual miners. It also receives and verifies the solutions submitted by the miners.

2. Stratum Protocol: The Stratum protocol is used by the pool server to communicate with the miners. It provides a standardized way of distributing work and receiving solutions.

3. Mining Software: Each miner in the pool runs their own mining software that connects to the pool server and receives work. The mining software also performs the calculations required to solve the block and submits the solution to the pool server.

4. Block Reward Distribution System: The block reward distribution system is responsible for dividing the reward among the pool members. There are several different methods for doing this, including proportional, PPLNS (Pay Per Last N Shares), and others.

Advantages of Mining Pools Mining pools offer several advantages over individual mining, including:

1. Increased Chances of Earning a Reward: By combining their computational power, miners in a pool have a greater chance of solving a block and earning a reward.

2. More Stable Income: Pool mining provides a more stable income stream than solo mining. Even if a miner does not solve a block, they will still receive a share of the reward.

3. Lower Variance: With pool mining, the variance in income is lower than solo mining, which can be important for miners who rely on a steady income from mining.

Disadvantages of Mining Pools While there are several advantages to mining pools, there are also some disadvantages to consider, including:

1. Pool Fees: Mining pools charge a fee for their services, typically a percentage of the reward earned. This can reduce the overall profitability of mining.

2. Centralization: By joining a mining pool, miners are essentially trusting the pool operator to distribute the rewards fairly. This can lead to centralization of the network and potential issues with trust.

3. Potential for Pool Hopping: Some miners may "pool hop" or switch between pools to maximize their profits. This can lead to instability in the pool and reduced profitability for other members.

Conclusion Mining pools have become an important part of the Bitcoin mining ecosystem, allowing individual miners to combine their resources and increase their chances of earning a reward. While there are advantages to pool mining, there are also some drawbacks that must be considered. Overall, mining pools provide a way for individual miners to participate in the Bitcoin network and earn rewards, even if they don't have the resources to compete on their own.

Cloud mining and its risks

Cloud mining is a type of mining where users can rent hash power from a third-party provider to mine cryptocurrencies such as Bitcoin. It has become popular in recent years, as it allows individuals to participate in mining without having to invest in expensive hardware and infrastructure.

However, cloud mining also comes with certain risks and disadvantages. In this section, we will discuss some of these risks and what users should consider before engaging in cloud mining.

1. Lack of control over mining hardware

When mining in the cloud, users do not have control over the mining hardware. They are essentially renting hash power from a third-party provider, which means they have no say in the type of hardware that is being used or how it is being operated.

This lack of control can be a disadvantage, as users have no way of verifying the quality or performance of the hardware. Additionally, if the provider experiences any issues with their hardware, users may experience downtime or reduced mining profits.

2. Dependency on the provider

Cloud mining also involves a significant degree of dependency on the provider. Users are reliant on the provider to operate the mining hardware and maintain the infrastructure required for mining. If the provider experiences any issues, such as power outages or network disruptions, it can have a direct impact on the user's mining profits.

Additionally, users must trust the provider to be honest and transparent in their operations. There have been cases of fraudulent cloud mining providers who have taken users' money without providing the promised hash power or returns.

3. Limited profitability

Cloud mining is typically less profitable than traditional mining, as users must pay fees to the provider for the hash power they rent. These fees can eat into profits significantly, and users may not be able to mine enough cryptocurrency to cover the costs of the rental fees.

Furthermore, the fees associated with cloud mining can be quite high, particularly if the provider is offering a guaranteed return or a fixed payout. Users should be cautious of any provider that promises high returns with little risk, as it may be too good to be true.

4. Security risks

Cloud mining also comes with certain security risks. Users must trust the provider to handle their personal and financial information securely, as well as keep their mining earnings safe.

There have been cases where cloud mining providers have been hacked, resulting in the loss of user data or funds. Users should ensure that any provider they choose has a strong security record and takes measures to protect user data and funds.

5. Lack of flexibility

Finally, cloud mining is typically less flexible than traditional mining. Users are limited in their ability to customize their mining setup or adjust their mining strategies. They must rely on the provider to handle these tasks for them, which can limit their profitability and mining efficiency.

In conclusion, cloud mining can be a viable option for those looking to participate in mining without investing in hardware and infrastructure. However, it comes with significant risks and limitations that users should be aware of. Users should conduct thorough research before engaging in cloud mining and choose a reputable provider with a strong track record.

Chapter 3: Mining Economics and Profitability
The costs of mining Bitcoin

Bitcoin mining is a complex and energy-intensive process that involves using powerful computers to solve complex mathematical problems. These problems are designed to secure the Bitcoin network and ensure the integrity of transactions, and as such, mining plays a crucial role in the functioning of the cryptocurrency. However, mining also comes with significant costs, both in terms of hardware and electricity, which can have a significant impact on profitability.

Hardware Costs:

One of the primary costs of Bitcoin mining is the hardware required to perform the computational tasks necessary to secure the network. In the early days of Bitcoin, miners could use standard desktop computers or even laptops to mine Bitcoin. However, as the network has grown and become more secure, the difficulty of mining has increased, and specialized hardware known as ASICs (application-specific integrated circuits) has become necessary.

These ASICs are specifically designed to perform the calculations required for Bitcoin mining, and they are significantly more efficient than traditional computer hardware. However, they are also expensive, with top-of-the-line ASICs costing thousands of dollars per unit. Additionally, ASICs become obsolete relatively quickly as the network's difficulty increases, meaning that miners must continually upgrade their equipment to stay competitive.

Electricity Costs:

Another significant cost of Bitcoin mining is electricity. Mining requires a massive amount of computational power, which in turn requires a significant amount of electricity to run. In fact, the Bitcoin network's energy consumption is estimated to be higher than that of some small countries.

Electricity costs can vary widely depending on location, with some areas having much lower electricity rates than others. However, even in areas with low rates, mining can still be expensive, as the amount of electricity required to run ASICs 24/7 is significant.

Other Costs:

In addition to hardware and electricity costs, there are several other expenses that miners must consider when calculating profitability. These include:

- Maintenance costs: ASICs require regular maintenance, and in some cases, repairs or replacements may be necessary.

- Cooling costs: ASICs generate a significant amount of heat, and as such, they require specialized cooling systems to prevent overheating.

- Mining pool fees: Many miners choose to join mining pools, which allow them to combine their resources and increase their chances of earning rewards. However, mining pools typically charge fees for their services.

Calculating Profitability:

Given the significant costs associated with mining, profitability is a crucial consideration for miners. To determine profitability, miners must consider several factors, including the cost of hardware and electricity, the current mining difficulty, and the price of Bitcoin.

There are several online calculators available that can help miners estimate their profitability based on these factors. However, it's important to remember that these calculations are only estimates and may not accurately reflect actual profits. Additionally, the price of Bitcoin is notoriously volatile, and sudden drops in price can significantly impact profitability.

Conclusion:

In summary, the costs of Bitcoin mining can be significant, with hardware and electricity expenses being the primary considerations. As such, miners must carefully consider these costs when deciding whether to enter the mining market and which hardware to purchase. While profitability can be challenging to calculate accurately, it remains a crucial consideration for miners looking to earn rewards for securing the Bitcoin network.

Calculating mining profitability

Calculating mining profitability is a crucial aspect of any miner's strategy, as it helps them determine if their mining operations are profitable or not. In this chapter, we will explore the different factors that go into calculating mining profitability.

Mining profitability can be determined by considering three key variables: mining hardware, mining difficulty, and electricity cost. Let's explore each of these variables in more detail:

Mining Hardware: Mining hardware is an essential part of mining profitability, and selecting the right hardware is critical for success. ASICs (Application-Specific Integrated Circuits) are the most commonly used mining hardware, and they are designed to perform specific hashing functions that are necessary for Bitcoin mining. ASICs are typically more expensive than other types of mining hardware, but they are also more efficient and can generate a higher hashrate, which means more mining rewards.

Mining Difficulty: Mining difficulty refers to the level of competition among miners to solve a block on the Bitcoin network. As more miners join the network, the difficulty level increases, and it becomes harder to mine Bitcoin. Conversely, when miners leave the network, the difficulty level decreases, and it becomes easier to mine Bitcoin. Mining difficulty is adjusted every 2016 blocks, which is roughly every two weeks, to ensure that new blocks are generated at a consistent rate of one every ten minutes.

Electricity Cost: Electricity cost is another crucial factor that affects mining profitability, as it is one of the primary ongoing costs of running a mining operation. The cost of electricity varies widely depending on location, with some regions having significantly lower electricity costs than others. Miners typically look for regions with low electricity costs to set up their mining operations, as it can significantly impact profitability.

To calculate mining profitability, miners use a profitability calculator that takes into account the cost of their mining hardware, the mining difficulty, and the electricity cost in their region. The calculator then estimates the miner's potential revenue and compares it to their ongoing costs to determine if the mining operation is profitable.

It's essential to note that mining profitability can change rapidly, and miners need to stay up to date on changes in mining difficulty and Bitcoin's price to adjust their operations accordingly. Additionally, it's crucial to consider the potential risks associated with mining, such as hardware failures or changes in regulatory policies that can impact mining profitability.

In conclusion, calculating mining profitability is a crucial aspect of any mining operation. By considering factors such as mining hardware, mining difficulty, and electricity cost, miners can determine their potential revenue and ongoing costs to determine if their operations are profitable. While mining profitability can change rapidly, staying informed on the latest developments in the mining industry can help miners adjust their operations and stay profitable over the long term.

Factors that impact mining profitability

Mining profitability is impacted by a variety of factors, some of which are within a miner's control, and others which are outside of their control. In this section, we will discuss the main factors that impact mining profitability.

1. Mining Difficulty

Mining difficulty is one of the most critical factors that impact mining profitability. The Bitcoin protocol automatically adjusts the difficulty of mining every 2016 blocks, which is roughly every two weeks. This adjustment is based on the total hash rate of the network, and the goal is to keep the block time at around 10 minutes. When the total hash rate increases, the mining difficulty also increases, which means that miners need to use more computational power to solve the cryptographic puzzle required to create a block. This increased computational power translates into higher electricity costs and hardware expenses, which ultimately reduces mining profitability.

2. Electricity Costs

Electricity costs are another significant factor that impacts mining profitability. The cost of electricity varies depending on the region, but it is generally one of the most significant expenses for miners. The amount of electricity that miners use is directly proportional to the hash rate of their mining equipment. As mining difficulty increases, so does the amount of electricity required to mine a block. Miners need to be aware of the cost of electricity in their region and choose a location where electricity costs are low.

3. Hardware Costs

Hardware costs are another significant expense for miners. The cost of mining hardware varies depending on the type of equipment used and the manufacturer. Some of the most popular mining hardware includes ASICs (Application-Specific Integrated Circuits) and GPUs (Graphics Processing Units). ASICs are more expensive than GPUs but are generally more efficient at mining Bitcoin. Miners need to carefully consider the cost of hardware and choose equipment that offers the best balance between cost and efficiency.

4. Mining Pool Fees

Mining pools are groups of miners who combine their computational power to mine Bitcoin more efficiently. Mining pool operators charge a fee for their services, which is usually a percentage of the block reward. These fees can vary depending on the pool, and they can have a significant impact on mining profitability.

5. Transaction Fees

Transaction fees are another factor that can impact mining profitability. Bitcoin transactions have a fee that is paid to miners for including the transaction in a block. The amount of the fee varies depending on the size of the transaction and the level of network congestion. As the Bitcoin network becomes more congested, transaction fees can increase, which can increase mining profitability.

6. Price of Bitcoin

The price of Bitcoin is perhaps the most significant factor that impacts mining profitability. The block reward is fixed at 6.25 BTC per block, but the value of Bitcoin can fluctuate dramatically. When the price of Bitcoin increases, mining profitability also increases. However, when the price of Bitcoin decreases, mining profitability can decline. Miners need to be aware of the market conditions and adjust their mining strategies accordingly.

Conclusion

Mining profitability is impacted by a variety of factors, some of which are within a miner's control, and others which are outside of their control. To maximize profitability, miners need to carefully consider the cost of hardware, electricity, and mining pool fees. They also need to monitor the market conditions and adjust their mining strategies accordingly. By doing so, they can ensure that they are earning the most Bitcoin possible for their efforts.

Long-term mining incentives and the halving

Bitcoin mining is a dynamic and evolving process that is influenced by various factors, including the long-term incentives offered by the network. In this section, we will explore the concept of long-term mining incentives and how they are impacted by an event known as the "halving."

Bitcoin has a finite supply of 21 million coins, and the rate at which new coins are created is gradually reduced over time. This reduction in the rate of new coin creation is achieved through a mechanism called the halving, which occurs approximately every four years.

During the halving event, the reward for mining a new block on the Bitcoin network is cut in half. This means that miners receive fewer bitcoins as a reward for their efforts, and it also reduces the overall supply of new bitcoins entering circulation. The halving is designed to ensure that the supply of bitcoin remains scarce, which helps to maintain its value over time.

The first halving occurred in 2012 when the block reward was reduced from 50 bitcoins to 25 bitcoins. The second halving occurred in 2016 when the block reward was reduced from 25 bitcoins to 12.5 bitcoins. The most recent halving occurred in May 2020, which reduced the block reward from 12.5 bitcoins to 6.25 bitcoins.

The halving has a significant impact on mining profitability, as it reduces the number of new bitcoins that miners can earn for their efforts. This reduction in the block reward is an essential factor that miners need to consider when calculating their profitability.

Miners who rely heavily on the income generated from mining new coins may be impacted more significantly by the halving. Those who have high operational costs and cannot adjust their operations quickly may struggle to remain profitable after the halving event.

As the block reward continues to decrease over time, miners will need to rely increasingly on transaction fees to maintain profitability. Transaction fees are collected by miners for verifying transactions and adding them to the blockchain, and they are an essential source of revenue for miners after the block reward is reduced.

One potential effect of the halving is that it could lead to a consolidation of the mining industry. As the profitability of mining decreases, smaller, less efficient miners may be forced out of the market. This could lead to a concentration of mining power in the hands of larger, more efficient miners, which could pose a risk to the decentralization of the network.

In summary, the halving is an essential event that affects the long-term mining incentives on the Bitcoin network. As the block reward continues to decrease, miners will need to rely increasingly on transaction fees to maintain profitability. The halving event can have a significant impact on mining profitability, and it may also lead to a consolidation of the mining industry over time.

Chapter 4: The Environmental Impact of Bitcoin Mining

Energy consumption and carbon emissions

Bitcoin mining has been the subject of significant criticism in recent years due to its high energy consumption and environmental impact. As of 2021, the Bitcoin network consumes approximately 116 terawatt-hours (TWh) of energy per year, which is equivalent to the annual energy consumption of countries like Argentina or the Netherlands. This level of energy consumption has led to concerns about the carbon footprint and environmental impact of Bitcoin mining.

The primary reason for Bitcoin's high energy consumption is the computational power required to solve the cryptographic puzzles necessary to add new blocks to the blockchain. Bitcoin mining involves using specialized computer hardware called ASICs (application-specific integrated circuits) to perform complex calculations in a process known as proof-of-work (PoW). Miners compete to solve these calculations, and the first miner to solve the puzzle is rewarded with newly created Bitcoins.

The energy consumption of Bitcoin mining can be attributed to several factors. First, the ASICs used in Bitcoin mining are highly specialized and energy-intensive to manufacture. Second, the machines run 24/7, consuming energy constantly. Third, the mining process is designed to become progressively more difficult over time, requiring ever-increasing amounts of computational power and energy to mine new blocks.

The high energy consumption of Bitcoin mining has led to concerns about its carbon footprint. The majority of Bitcoin mining takes place in China, where coal-fired power plants are still a significant source of electricity. As a result, estimates suggest that the carbon footprint of Bitcoin mining in China alone is equivalent to that of the entire country of New Zealand.

However, it is worth noting that not all Bitcoin mining is created equal in terms of energy consumption and environmental impact. Some mining operations use renewable energy sources, such as hydroelectric or solar power, to power their operations. Additionally, as the price of Bitcoin continues to rise, it becomes more economically feasible for mining operations to invest in renewable energy sources.

There are also efforts underway to improve the energy efficiency of Bitcoin mining. For example, some mining operations are experimenting with using more energy-efficient hardware or repurposing waste heat generated by mining machines for other purposes, such as heating buildings. Additionally, some cryptocurrency projects are exploring alternative consensus mechanisms to proof-of-work, such as proof-of-stake (PoS), which require significantly less energy to operate.

In conclusion, the high energy consumption of Bitcoin mining is a legitimate concern from an environmental standpoint. However, it is important to consider the nuances of the issue and the efforts underway to mitigate the environmental impact of Bitcoin mining. As the cryptocurrency industry continues to evolve, it is likely that we will see further developments in the area of energy-efficient mining and alternative consensus mechanisms.

Renewable energy and its role in Bitcoin mining

As the global concern about climate change and carbon emissions grows, there has been increasing scrutiny of the energy consumption and carbon footprint of Bitcoin mining. The Bitcoin network currently consumes a significant amount of energy, with estimates suggesting that the annual energy consumption of Bitcoin mining is comparable to that of a mid-sized country like Argentina or Norway. This has led to concerns about the environmental impact of Bitcoin mining, and calls for the industry to transition to more sustainable sources of energy.

One potential solution to the energy consumption problem is the use of renewable energy sources such as solar, wind, and hydroelectric power. Renewable energy has several advantages over traditional energy sources such as coal and natural gas, including lower carbon emissions, lower operating costs, and lower dependence on fossil fuels.

Several Bitcoin mining companies have already started to explore the use of renewable energy sources. For example, in May 2021, the North American Bitcoin mining company Riot Blockchain announced that it was expanding its mining operations to a new facility in Texas that would be powered by 100% renewable energy. The company plans to use a mix of solar and wind power to generate electricity for its mining operations.

Similarly, the Bitcoin mining company Bitfarms recently signed an agreement with a hydroelectric power plant in Quebec, Canada, to purchase electricity at a reduced rate. The company plans to use the cheap hydroelectric power to expand its mining operations in the region.

There are also several initiatives underway to promote the use of renewable energy in Bitcoin mining. For example, the Crypto Climate Accord, a coalition of organizations in the crypto industry, has set a goal of making the industry 100% powered by renewable energy by 2025. The initiative aims to bring together companies, investors, and governments to accelerate the transition to renewable energy sources.

In addition to reducing the environmental impact of Bitcoin mining, the use of renewable energy sources could also make mining more profitable for miners. Renewable energy sources such as solar and wind power are often cheaper than traditional energy sources, which could help to reduce mining costs and increase profits.

However, there are also several challenges associated with the use of renewable energy sources in Bitcoin mining. One of the biggest challenges is the intermittent nature of renewable energy sources. Solar and wind power are dependent on weather conditions, and their output can vary significantly from day to day or even hour to hour. This can make it difficult to maintain a stable and reliable source of electricity for mining operations.

To address this challenge, some mining companies are exploring the use of energy storage solutions such as batteries or pumped hydro storage. These technologies can help to store excess energy generated during periods of high output, and release it during periods of low output or high demand.

Another challenge is the availability of renewable energy sources in different regions. Solar and wind power, for example, are more abundant in certain regions than others, and the availability of these energy sources can vary depending on the time of day or year. This can make it difficult for mining companies to rely solely on renewable energy sources, and may require them to supplement with traditional energy sources.

Overall, the use of renewable energy sources in Bitcoin mining has the potential to address the environmental concerns associated with the industry, while also making mining more profitable for miners. However, there are also several challenges that need to be addressed to make this transition a reality. As the industry continues to evolve, it will be important for mining companies, investors, and governments to work together to accelerate the adoption of renewable energy sources and make Bitcoin mining a more sustainable and environmentally friendly industry.

Criticisms and misconceptions about Bitcoin mining's environmental impact

Bitcoin mining has been a subject of controversy due to its perceived negative environmental impact. While it is true that Bitcoin mining consumes a significant amount of energy, there are also many misconceptions and criticisms that are not entirely accurate. In this chapter, we will examine some of these criticisms and misconceptions and provide a more nuanced view of the environmental impact of Bitcoin mining.

One of the most common criticisms of Bitcoin mining is that it consumes too much energy and contributes to climate change. While it is true that Bitcoin mining consumes energy, it is important to consider where that energy comes from. Many Bitcoin miners use renewable energy sources such as hydropower, wind power, and solar power. In fact, a 2021 study by the Cambridge Center for Alternative Finance found that 39% of Bitcoin mining energy comes from renewable sources, and the trend is growing. Additionally, renewable energy is becoming more affordable, making it an increasingly attractive option for miners.

Another criticism of Bitcoin mining is that it is wasteful and has no real-world value. This argument fails to recognize the intrinsic value of Bitcoin as a decentralized, trustless, and censorship-resistant store of value. Bitcoin has real-world value because it allows people to store and transfer wealth without the need for a trusted third party. This is particularly important for people living in countries with unstable governments or economies, where traditional banking systems may not be trustworthy.

Some people also argue that Bitcoin mining is a threat to the stability of the power grid because it puts too much strain on the system. While it is true that Bitcoin mining can require a significant amount of energy, miners typically operate in areas with excess energy capacity. In some cases, Bitcoin mining operations have even helped to stabilize the power grid by providing a reliable source of demand for excess energy.

Another criticism of Bitcoin mining is that it contributes to e-waste because mining hardware becomes obsolete quickly. While it is true that mining hardware can become obsolete, miners have an incentive to recycle and reuse old hardware because it is still valuable for mining other cryptocurrencies. Additionally, many mining hardware manufacturers have implemented recycling programs to reduce e-waste.

Finally, some people argue that Bitcoin mining is a Ponzi scheme or a bubble that will eventually collapse, making all the energy and resources put into mining worthless. This argument fails to recognize that Bitcoin has been around for over a decade and has proven to be a resilient and valuable asset. While the price of Bitcoin may be volatile, it has consistently grown in value over the long term.

In conclusion, while it is true that Bitcoin mining consumes a significant amount of energy, there are many misconceptions and criticisms of its environmental impact that are not entirely accurate. By using renewable energy, contributing to the stability of the power grid, and recycling old mining hardware, Bitcoin mining can be a sustainable and valuable activity. It is important to approach the environmental impact of Bitcoin mining with a nuanced understanding of its benefits and drawbacks.

Chapter 5: Alternative Consensus Mechanisms Overview of proof-of-stake and other consensus algorithms

Bitcoin mining relies on a consensus mechanism known as proof-of-work (PoW), which is designed to be secure and resistant to attack. However, PoW also requires a significant amount of energy consumption, which has led to concerns about its environmental impact. As a result, alternative consensus mechanisms have emerged that seek to provide a more energy-efficient and sustainable way to secure blockchain networks. One such alternative is proof-of-stake (PoS), which works differently from PoW and has gained popularity in recent years. In this chapter, we will explore PoS and other alternative consensus mechanisms.

Proof-of-Stake (PoS)

PoS is a consensus mechanism that uses a different method to validate transactions and create new blocks. Instead of miners solving complex mathematical problems, validators are selected based on the amount of cryptocurrency they hold and are willing to "stake" or lock up as collateral. The higher the stake, the higher the chance of being selected to validate transactions and earn rewards. This means that PoS networks are secured by those who have the most to lose, as they are incentivized to behave honestly to avoid losing their stake.

There are several benefits to using PoS over PoW. First, PoS networks consume significantly less energy than PoW networks because there is no need for miners to compete to solve complex mathematical problems. Second, PoS networks are less susceptible to 51% attacks, as an attacker would need to control a majority of the network's staked coins rather than a majority of the computing power. Finally, PoS networks are generally more decentralized than PoW networks, as they do not require specialized hardware and can be run on standard computers.

One of the most popular PoS networks is Ethereum 2.0, which is currently in the process of transitioning from PoW to PoS. This transition is expected to significantly reduce the network's energy consumption while still maintaining its security.

Other Consensus Mechanisms

In addition to PoS, there are several other alternative consensus mechanisms that have been proposed or are currently in use.

Delegated Proof-of-Stake (DPoS) is a variant of PoS that uses a voting system to elect a small number of delegates who are responsible for validating transactions and creating new blocks. This system is designed to be more efficient and scalable than PoS, as it reduces the number of validators needed to secure the network.

Proof-of-Authority (PoA) is a consensus mechanism that relies on a trusted group of validators who are authorized to create new blocks. This mechanism is commonly used in private blockchain networks where trust is already established.

Proof-of-Elapsed-Time (PoET) is a consensus mechanism that uses a random wait time to select the next validator. This method is designed to be energy-efficient and is used in the Hyperledger Sawtooth blockchain platform.

Proof-of-Burn (PoB) is a consensus mechanism that requires users to send cryptocurrency to a burn address to prove their commitment to the network. This method is designed to discourage malicious behavior by making it costly to attack the network.

Conclusion

Proof-of-stake and other alternative consensus mechanisms offer promising alternatives to the energy-intensive proof-of-work consensus mechanism used by Bitcoin and other cryptocurrencies. PoS networks are generally more energy-efficient, more secure against 51% attacks, and more decentralized than PoW networks. While there are still some challenges to overcome, such as ensuring fair distribution of coins and preventing centralization, these alternative consensus mechanisms offer a glimpse of a more sustainable future for blockchain networks.

Advantages and disadvantages of alternative consensus mechanisms

Bitcoin's consensus mechanism, known as proof-of-work, has been the backbone of the network since its inception. However, other consensus mechanisms, such as proof-of-stake, have emerged as potential alternatives. In this section, we will discuss the advantages and disadvantages of alternative consensus mechanisms.

Advantages of Alternative Consensus Mechanisms:

1. Lower Energy Consumption: Proof-of-work consensus algorithms require an enormous amount of computational power to solve complex mathematical problems. As a result, they require a significant amount of energy to operate. Proof-of-stake, on the other hand, is a more energy-efficient consensus mechanism that operates using a different approach. In proof-of-stake, validators are required to hold a certain amount of cryptocurrency in a special wallet as collateral. This helps to prevent centralization and also reduces energy consumption.

2. More Secure: Proof-of-stake is more secure than proof-of-work in some respects. In proof-of-work, miners can manipulate the network by obtaining a majority of the network's computational power. In contrast, proof-of-stake

ensures that validators have a stake in the network and are incentivized to act in its best interests.

3. Easier to Join: Joining a proof-of-work network requires expensive hardware, technical expertise, and a significant amount of capital to cover operating costs. In contrast, proof-of-stake requires much less capital investment and technical expertise to operate.

Disadvantages of Alternative Consensus Mechanisms:

1. Centralization: Proof-of-stake can be vulnerable to centralization if a few validators hold a large amount of the cryptocurrency required to participate in the network. This could result in the network being controlled by a small group of validators.

2. Less Decentralized: Some argue that proof-of-stake is less decentralized than proof-of-work. In proof-of-work, anyone can participate in the network as long as they have the required hardware and computational power. In contrast, proof-of-stake requires validators to hold a certain amount of cryptocurrency. This means that the network could be controlled by a smaller group of validators.

3. Difficult to Implement: Implementing proof-of-stake requires significant changes to the network's code and consensus rules. This can be a difficult and time-consuming

process, and it can also introduce new vulnerabilities into the network.

In conclusion, while proof-of-work has been the dominant consensus mechanism in the blockchain industry, proof-of-stake and other alternatives are gaining popularity due to their advantages over proof-of-work. However, these alternative consensus mechanisms also have their own set of challenges that need to be addressed to ensure their long-term viability.

Potential future developments in blockchain consensus

As the world of blockchain and cryptocurrencies continues to evolve, there are a number of potential developments in consensus mechanisms that could change the way that transactions are verified and validated on the network. Here are some of the most promising possibilities:

1. Proof-of-stake (PoS) improvements: While PoS has already emerged as a popular alternative to proof-of-work (PoW) in a number of blockchain networks, there is still room for improvement in this area. Some researchers are exploring new ways to distribute rewards and penalties to PoS participants, in order to encourage greater network security and prevent attacks by malicious actors.

2. Hybrid consensus models: As mentioned earlier, there are already some blockchain networks that use hybrid consensus models, combining PoW and PoS or other mechanisms. However, these models are still relatively new and untested, and there is plenty of room for further experimentation in this area. For example, some researchers are exploring the potential for combining PoS and directed acyclic graph (DAG) technologies to create a more scalable and secure consensus model.

3. Delegated Proof of Stake (DPoS): DPoS is a consensus mechanism where token holders vote on a group of delegates to validate transactions on the network. These delegates are responsible for validating transactions and receive rewards for doing so. DPoS has the potential to increase network efficiency and scalability, but it also raises concerns about centralization and voting power.

4. Byzantine fault tolerance (BFT): BFT is a consensus mechanism that allows a distributed network to reach consensus even in the face of malicious actors. While BFT has been around for some time, it has gained renewed interest in the context of blockchain and cryptocurrencies, and there are a number of projects exploring how this mechanism could be used to enhance network security and scalability.

5. Sharding: Sharding is a technique for dividing a blockchain network into smaller, more manageable pieces called shards. This can improve network performance and scalability, but it also raises concerns about security and data privacy. Some researchers are exploring the potential for combining sharding with other consensus mechanisms to create a more robust and secure network.

6. Zero-Knowledge Proof (ZKP): Zero-Knowledge Proof is a method of validating transactions without

revealing the underlying data. This technique has the potential to enhance network privacy and security, but it also raises concerns about scalability and computation costs. Researchers are exploring ways to use ZKP in combination with other consensus mechanisms to create a more secure and efficient network.

Overall, there is still much to be discovered and developed in the field of blockchain consensus mechanisms. While PoW remains the dominant mechanism for many blockchain networks, there is a growing interest in exploring alternative models that can provide greater scalability, security, and efficiency. As the technology continues to evolve, we can expect to see a growing number of blockchain projects experimenting with new consensus mechanisms and exploring new ways to enhance the security, scalability, and overall performance of their networks.

Conclusion

Review of the book's key takeaways

As we conclude this book on Bitcoin mining, let's review some of the key takeaways from the previous chapters.

First and foremost, Bitcoin mining is a crucial process that ensures the security and integrity of the Bitcoin network. Miners are responsible for verifying transactions and adding new blocks to the blockchain, in exchange for block rewards and transaction fees.

Mining is a highly competitive process, and miners must constantly upgrade their hardware and software to stay ahead of the competition. Mining profitability is influenced by several factors, including the price of Bitcoin, mining difficulty, electricity costs, and hardware efficiency.

Mining pools and cloud mining services have become popular alternatives to solo mining, as they allow miners to combine their resources and share rewards. However, there are also risks involved in joining a mining pool or using cloud mining services, including the potential for centralization and fraud.

The environmental impact of Bitcoin mining has been a hotly debated topic, with some critics claiming that it consumes an excessive amount of energy and contributes to carbon emissions. However, others argue that Bitcoin mining can incentivize the development of renewable energy sources, and that the environmental impact of traditional financial systems is often overlooked.

Finally, alternative consensus mechanisms such as proof-of-stake are being developed as potential solutions to the energy consumption and centralization concerns associated with proof-of-work. However, these alternative mechanisms also have their own advantages and disadvantages.

In conclusion, Bitcoin mining is a complex and constantly evolving field, with many challenges and opportunities. As the Bitcoin ecosystem continues to grow and mature, it will be fascinating to see how mining and consensus mechanisms continue to evolve and adapt to new technologies and demands.

Final thoughts on the importance of Bitcoin mining

Bitcoin mining is a critical component of the cryptocurrency's infrastructure, and it plays a significant role in maintaining the integrity and security of the blockchain network. While mining has faced criticism due to its energy consumption and environmental impact, it remains a vital aspect of the blockchain's success. In this final section, we will review the importance of Bitcoin mining and its potential for the future.

First and foremost, Bitcoin mining is essential for maintaining the integrity of the network. Miners are responsible for verifying and processing transactions, ensuring that they are accurate and legitimate. Without mining, the blockchain would be vulnerable to manipulation, and the system would be unreliable.

Secondly, mining plays a critical role in the security of the network. The proof-of-work algorithm used by Bitcoin ensures that miners must solve complex mathematical equations to create new blocks. This process requires significant computational power, making it difficult and costly for attackers to manipulate the network. As a result, the blockchain is highly resistant to fraud, making it a trusted and secure platform for users to conduct transactions.

In addition to its essential role in maintaining the network's integrity and security, Bitcoin mining has significant economic implications. Miners are rewarded with newly minted Bitcoin and transaction fees, which incentivizes them to continue to secure the network. This reward system has created a competitive market for mining, with miners constantly searching for ways to increase their efficiency and reduce costs.

The mining industry has also created a demand for specialized hardware and software, providing opportunities for technological innovation and development. The competition among mining hardware manufacturers has led to the creation of increasingly powerful and efficient equipment, making mining more accessible and profitable for individuals and companies.

However, the environmental impact of Bitcoin mining cannot be ignored. The significant energy consumption required to power the mining process has led to concerns about the industry's sustainability. As we have discussed in earlier chapters, there are efforts to make mining more energy-efficient, such as through the use of renewable energy sources and the development of alternative consensus mechanisms. Nonetheless, the environmental impact of mining remains a critical issue that must be addressed moving forward.

Looking to the future, there are opportunities for further innovation and development in the mining industry. As the demand for Bitcoin and other cryptocurrencies continues to grow, so too will the need for secure and reliable mining operations. The continued development of specialized hardware and software, as well as alternative consensus mechanisms, will be critical in meeting these demands.

Furthermore, the potential use cases for blockchain technology continue to expand beyond cryptocurrency. From supply chain management to digital identity verification, the blockchain offers a secure and transparent platform for a wide range of applications. As these use cases grow, the importance of maintaining a secure and reliable blockchain network will only increase.

In conclusion, Bitcoin mining is a critical component of the cryptocurrency ecosystem, providing a secure and reliable platform for users to conduct transactions. While the industry faces challenges related to its environmental impact, the potential for further innovation and development offers opportunities for a more sustainable and efficient mining industry. As blockchain technology continues to evolve and expand, the importance of maintaining a secure and reliable network will only become more significant, making Bitcoin mining an essential aspect of the digital economy.

Encouragement to learn more and get involved in the Bitcoin community

As we come to the end of this book, it is clear that Bitcoin mining is an incredibly important and fascinating aspect of the Bitcoin network. We have explored the basics of how Bitcoin mining works, the economics and profitability of mining, the environmental impact of mining, and the potential for alternative consensus mechanisms to emerge.

However, it is important to note that this is just the beginning. The world of Bitcoin and blockchain technology is constantly evolving and there is always more to learn. If you have found this book interesting and informative, we encourage you to continue learning about Bitcoin and to get involved in the Bitcoin community.

One great way to learn more about Bitcoin is to attend local Bitcoin meetups or conferences. These events are a great opportunity to meet like-minded individuals, learn from experts in the field, and even get hands-on experience with Bitcoin mining hardware.

Another way to get involved in the Bitcoin community is to contribute to open-source Bitcoin projects. There are many projects that are in need of developers, designers, and other contributors. By getting involved in these projects, you can not only learn more about Bitcoin, but also help to make the Bitcoin ecosystem stronger and more secure.

Finally, it is important to remember that Bitcoin and blockchain technology have the potential to transform the world in many positive ways. From providing access to financial services for the unbanked to enabling new forms of peer-to-peer collaboration, Bitcoin has the potential to empower individuals and communities around the world.

As you continue to learn about Bitcoin and blockchain technology, we encourage you to keep an open mind and to think critically about the potential benefits and risks of these technologies. By doing so, you can help to ensure that Bitcoin and blockchain technology are used in ways that promote greater financial and social equality, transparency, and innovation.

THE END

Key Terms and Definitions

To help you better understand the language and concepts related to aging and older adults, below you will find a list of key terms and their definitions.

Key Terms

Bitcoin mining: The process of adding new transactions to the Bitcoin blockchain by solving complex mathematical equations using computer hardware.

Blockchain: A digital ledger that records and stores all Bitcoin transactions.

Hash rate: The speed at which a miner can compute the mathematical equations required to add a new block to the blockchain.

Proof of work: A consensus mechanism that requires miners to perform a certain amount of work in order to add a new block to the blockchain.

Mining pool: A group of miners who work together to increase their chances of successfully mining a block and sharing the rewards.

Cloud mining: A process where users can rent mining hardware and software from a remote provider.

Block reward: The amount of Bitcoin that is awarded to the miner who successfully adds a new block to the blockchain.

Mining difficulty: A measure of how difficult it is to mine a new block on the blockchain, adjusted automatically every 2016 blocks to maintain a target block time of 10 minutes.

ASIC: Application-specific integrated circuit, a specialized computer chip designed for the specific task of mining Bitcoin.

Mining profitability: The potential profit that a miner can earn based on the cost of hardware, electricity, and the current block reward.

Halving: The event that occurs every 210,000 blocks (approximately every four years) where the block reward is halved, reducing the amount of newly minted Bitcoin.

Proof of stake: A consensus mechanism that requires users to hold a certain amount of cryptocurrency in order to validate transactions and add new blocks to the blockchain.

Energy consumption: The amount of electricity required to power the hardware used in Bitcoin mining.

Carbon emissions: The amount of greenhouse gases emitted during the process of generating the electricity required for Bitcoin mining.

Renewable energy: Energy generated from sources that do not deplete natural resources, such as solar, wind, or hydroelectric power.

Centralization: The concentration of power and control in the hands of a small group of entities, potentially leading to issues of fairness, security, and censorship.

Decentralization: The distribution of power and control among a large number of entities, reducing the risk of centralized control and potential issues.

Supporting Materials

Introduction:

- Bitcoin. (2022). In Encyclopædia Britannica. https://www.britannica.com/topic/bitcoin

Chapter 1: The Basics of Bitcoin Mining:

- Antonopoulos, A. M. (2014). Mastering Bitcoin: Unlocking digital cryptocurrencies. O'Reilly Media, Inc.
- Nakamoto, S. (2008). Bitcoin: A peer-to-peer electronic cash system. https://bitcoin.org/bitcoin.pdf

Chapter 2: Mining Pools and Cloud Mining:

- Kroll, J. A., Davey, I. C., & Felten, E. W. (2013). The economics of Bitcoin mining, or Bitcoin in the presence of adversaries. Proceedings of WEIS, 2013. https://www.weusecoins.com/assets/pdf/library/The-Economics-of-Bitcoin-Mining-or-Bitcoin-in-the-Presence-of-Adversaries.pdf
- Rosenfeld, M. (2011). Analysis of Bitcoin pooled mining reward systems. arXiv preprint arXiv:1112.4980. https://arxiv.org/abs/1112.4980

Chapter 3: Mining Economics and Profitability:

- Cocco, L., Concas, G., & Marchesi, M. (2018). Modeling and simulation of the economics of mining in the Bitcoin market. Future Generation Computer Systems, 81, 721-733. https://doi.org/10.1016/j.future.2017.11.022

- Hayes, A. S. (2019). A cost of production model for Bitcoin. https://www.bitcoin.kn/wp-content/uploads/2019/05/hayes_model.pdf

Chapter 4: The Environmental Impact of Bitcoin Mining:

- Krause, M., & Tolaymat, T. (2018). Quantification of energy and carbon costs for mining cryptocurrencies. Nature Sustainability, 1(11), 711-718. https://doi.org/10.1038/s41893-018-0152-7

- Stoll, K., Klaaßen, L., & Gallersdörfer, U. (2021). Beyond the energy consumption debate: The impact of proof-of-work on the environment. Sustainability, 13(15), 8525. https://doi.org/10.3390/su13158525

Chapter 5: Alternative Consensus Mechanisms:

- Buterin, V. (2014). A next-generation smart contract and decentralized application platform. Ethereum White Paper. https://ethereum.org/en/whitepaper/

- Kiayias, A., Miller, A., & Zindros, D. (2017). Non-interactive proofs of proof-of-work. Proceedings of ACM CCS, 2017. https://eprint.iacr.org/2017/963.pdf

Conclusion:

- Narayanan, A., Bonneau, J., Felten, E., Miller, A., & Goldfeder, S. (2016). Bitcoin and Cryptocurrency Technologies: A Comprehensive Introduction. Princeton University Press.

- Swan, M. (2015). Blockchain: Blueprint for a new economy. O'Reilly Media, Inc.

www.ingramcontent.com/pod-product-compliance
Lightning Source LLC
LaVergne TN
LVHW021229080526
838199LV00089B/5959